Big Trucks

DIGGERS at Work

D. R. Addison

PowerKiDS press.
New York

For my little truck experts, Deming, Riley, and Hannah

Published in 2009 by The Rosen Publishing Group, Inc.
29 East 21st Street, New York, NY 10010

First Edition

Editor: Joanne Randolph
Book Design: Greg Tucker
Photo Research: Jessica Gerweck

Photo Credits: All images Shutterstock.com.

Library of Congress Cataloging-in-Publication Data

Addison, D. R.
Diggers at work / D. R. Addison. — 1st ed.
p. cm. — (Big trucks)
Includes index.
ISBN 978-1-4358-2700-4 (library binding) — ISBN 978-1-4358-3086-8 (pbk.)
ISBN 978-1-4358-3092-9 (6-pack)
1. Earthmoving machinery—Juvenile literature. I. Title.
TA725.A32 2009
621.8'65—dc22

2008021615

Manufactured in the United States of America

Contents

This is a digger, or excavator. Diggers work hard every day.

There are many kinds of diggers. This kind of digger is called a backhoe loader.

This is a giant digger. "Giant" means "really big."

Some diggers are small. This mini digger is used for smaller jobs.

Diggers have a shovel on the front. They use this to scoop, or dig.

The shovel has **teeth** on it. These teeth cut through dirt and rock.

Diggers can use different tools. This digger has a **claw** tool for picking up and holding things.

Time to get to work! This digger fills a **dump truck** with all the dirt it has dug up.

Diggers are used for many kinds of jobs. This digger is making a place to build a house.

330LC

Diggers help build and fix roads, too. Thanks, diggers, for working so hard every day!

Words to Know

claw

dump truck

teeth

Index

Web Sites

Due to the changing nature of Internet links, PowerKids Press has developed an online list of Web sites related to the subject of this book. This site is updated regularly. Please use this link to access the list:
www.powerkidslinks.com/bigt/digger/